MW01098273

Interactive Science Notebook: The Human Body

Authors: Schyrlet Cameron and Carolyn Craig

Editor: Mary Dieterich

Proofreaders: Margaret Brown and April Albert

COPYRIGHT © 2019 Mark Twain Media, Inc.

ISBN 978-1-62223-764-7

Printing No. CD-405030

Mark Twain Media, Inc., Publishers
Distributed by Carson-Dellosa Publishing LLC

Visit us at www.carsondellosa.com

Table of Contents

To the Teacher

Introduction 1

Organizing an Interactive Notebook.......... 2

Left-hand and Right-hand Notebook
Pages.. 3

Student Handouts

Interactive Science Notebook Grading
Rubric 4

Human Body Outline 5

**Interactive Notebook Cover:
The Human Body**

Student Instructions 6

Right-hand Page: Mini-Lesson.................. 7

Cover Cutouts 8

Lessons

Unit 1: Body Organization

The Human Cell 9

Cells, Tissues, Organs, and Systems 12

Unit 2: Skeletal and Muscular Systems

Skeletal System 15

Joints of the Human Body 18

Muscular System.................................... 21

Unit 3: Digestive and Excretory Systems

Digestive System 24

Excretory System................................... 27

Unit 4: Respiratory and Circulatory Systems

Respiratory System................................ 30

Circulatory System................................. 33

Unit 5: Lymphatic and Immune Systems

Lymphatic and Immune Systems 36

Unit 6: Nervous and Endocrine Systems

Nervous System..................................... 39

The Five Senses 42

Endocrine System.................................. 45

Unit 7: Reproductive System

Sexual Reproduction.............................. 48

Male and Female Reproductive
Systems.. 51

Genetics 54

Heredity... 57

The Developing Baby.............................. 60

Introduction

Interactive Science Notebook: The Human Body is designed to allow students to become active participants in their own learning. The book lays out an easy-to-follow plan for setting up, creating, and maintaining an interactive notebook.

An interactive notebook is simply a spiral notebook that students use to store and organize important information. It is a culmination of student work throughout the unit of study. Once completed, the notebook becomes the student's own personalized notebook and a great resource for reviewing and studying for tests.

The intent of the book is to help students make sense of new information. Textbooks often present more facts and data than students can process at one time. This book introduces each concept in an easy-to-read and easy-to-understand format that does not overwhelm the learner. The text presents only the most important information, making it easier for students to comprehend. Vocabulary words are printed in boldfaced type.

The Human Body contains 19 lessons covering 7 units of study: Body Organization, Skeletal and Muscular Systems, Digestive and Excretory Systems, Respiratory and Circulatory Systems, Lymphatic and Immune Systems, Nervous and Endocrine Systems, and the Reproductive System. The units can be used in the order presented or in an order that best fits the classroom curriculum. Teachers can easily differentiate units to address the individual learning levels and needs of students. The lessons are designed to support state and national standards. Each lesson consists of three pages.

- **Student Instruction page:** directions for creating the interactive page and for extending learning.
- **Input page (Mini-Lesson, Right-hand page):** essential information for understanding the lesson concepts.
- **Output page (Left-hand page):** hands-on activity such as a foldable or graphic organizer to help students process essential information from the lesson.

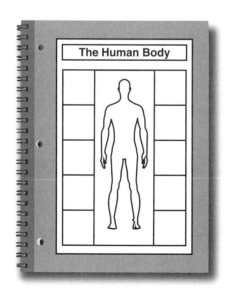
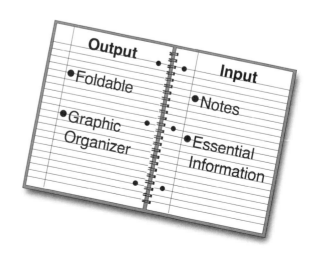

Organizing an Interactive Notebook

What Is an Interactive Notebook?

Does this sound familiar? "I can't find my homework…class notes…study guide." If so, the interactive notebook is a tool students can use to help manage this problem. An interactive notebook is simply a notebook that students use to record, store, and organize their work. The "interactive" aspect of the notebook comes from the fact that students are working with information in various ways as they fill in the notebook. Once completed, the notebook becomes the student's own personalized study guide and a great resource for reviewing information, reinforcing concepts, and studying for tests.

Materials Needed to Create an Interactive Notebook

- Notebook (spiral, composition, or binder with loose-leaf paper)
- Glue stick
- Scissors
- Colored pencils (we do not recommend using markers)
- Tabs

Creating an Interactive Notebook

A good time to introduce the interactive notebook is at the beginning of a new unit of study. Use the following steps to get started.

Step 1: *Notebook Cover*
Students design a cover to reflect the units of study (see pages 6–8). They should add their names and other important information as directed by the teacher.

Step 2: *Grading Rubric*
Take time to discuss the grading rubric with the students. It is important for each student to understand the expectations for creating the interactive notebook.

Step 3: *Table of Contents*
Students label the first several pages of the notebook "Table of Contents." When completing a new page, they then add its title to the table of contents.

Step 4: *Creating Pages*
The notebook is developed using the dual-page format. The right-hand side is the input page where essential information and notes from readings, lectures, or videos are placed. The left-hand side is the output page reserved for foldable activities, charts, graphic organizers, etc. Students number the front and back of each page in the bottom outside corner (odd: LEFT-side; even: RIGHT-side).

Step 5: *Tab Units*
Add a tab to the edge of the first page of each unit to make it easy to flip to that unit.

Step 6: *Glossary*
Reserve several pages at the back of the notebook where students can create a glossary of domain-specific terms encountered in each lesson.

Step 7: *Pocket*
Students need to attach a pocket to the inside of the back cover of the notebook for storage of handouts, returned quizzes, class syllabus, and other items that don't seem to belong on pages of the notebook. This can be an envelope, resealable plastic bag, or students can design their own pocket.

Left-hand and Right-hand Notebook Pages

Interactive notebooks are usually viewed open like a textbook. This allows the student to view the left-hand page and right-hand page at the same time. You have several options for how to format the two pages. Traditionally, the right-hand page is used as the input or the content part of the lesson. The left-hand page is the student output part of the lesson. This is where the students have an opportunity to show what they have learned in a creative and colorful way. (Color helps the brain remember information better.) The notebook image on the right details different types of items and activities that could be included for each page.

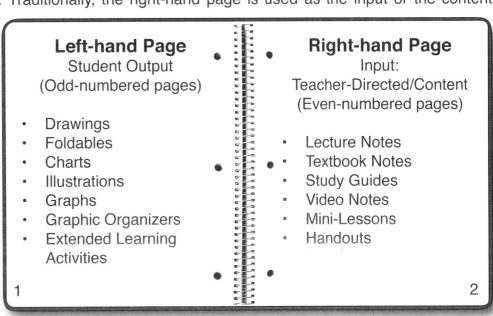

Left-hand Page
Student Output
(Odd-numbered pages)

- Drawings
- Foldables
- Charts
- Illustrations
- Graphs
- Graphic Organizers
- Extended Learning Activities

1

Right-hand Page
Input:
Teacher-Directed/Content
(Even-numbered pages)

- Lecture Notes
- Textbook Notes
- Study Guides
- Video Notes
- Mini-Lessons
- Handouts

2

The format of the interactive notebook involves both the right-brain and left-brain hemispheres to help students process information. When creating the pages, start with the left-hand page. First, have students date the page. Students then move to the right-hand page and the teacher-directed part of the lesson. Finally, students use the information they have learned to complete the left-hand page. Below is an example of completed right- and left-hand pages.

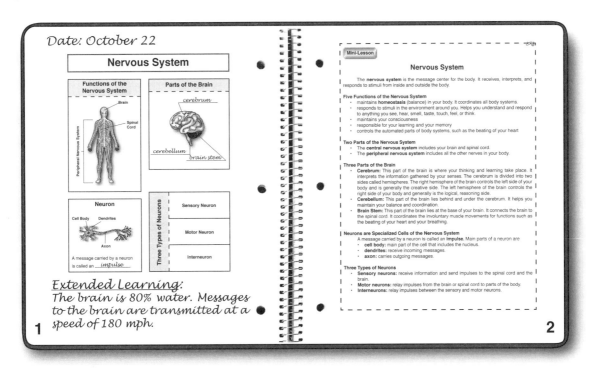

Interactive Science Notebook Grading Rubric

Directions: Review the criteria for the grading rubric that will be used to score your completed notebook. Place this page in your notebook.

Interactive Science Notebook Grading Rubric

Category	Excellent (4)	Good Work (3)	Needs Improvement (2)	Incomplete (1)
Table of Contents	Table of contents is complete.	Table of contents is mostly complete.	Table of contents is somewhat complete.	Attempt was made to include table of contents.
Organization	All notebook pages are in correct order. All are numbered, dated, and titled correctly.	Most pages are in correct order. Most are numbered, dated, and titled correctly.	Some pages are in correct order. Some are numbered, dated, or titled correctly.	Few pages are in correct order. Few are numbered, dated, or titled correctly.
Content	All information complete, accurate, and placed in the correct order. All spelling correct.	Most information complete, accurate, and placed in the correct order. Most spelling correct.	Some information complete, accurate, and placed in the correct order. Some spelling errors.	Few pages correctly completed. Many spelling errors.
Appearance	All notebook pages are neat and colorful.	Most notebook pages are neat and colorful.	Some notebook pages are neat and colorful.	Few notebook pages are neat and colorful.

Teacher's Comments:

Human Body Outline

Use this outline with any of the human body lessons to illustrate the systems of the human body.

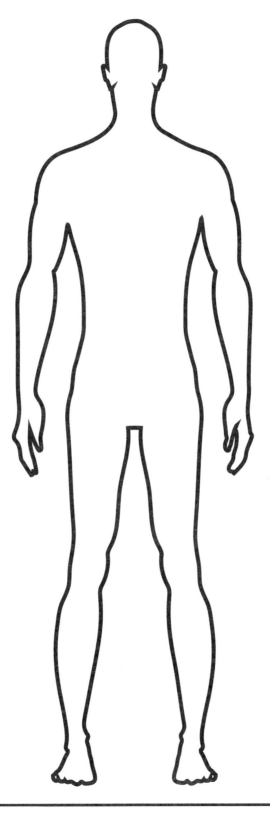

Student Instructions: The Human Body Notebook Cover

Materials Needed

Glue, scissors, colored pencils

How to Create a Right-hand Interactive Notebook Page

Read the Mini-Lesson page. Then cut out the page and attach it to the right-hand page of your interactive notebook. Use what you have learned to create the cover for your notebook.

How to Create Your Interactive Notebook Cover

Create a cover that will reflect the topics you will explore in your study of the human body.

Step 1: Use an online resource or your science textbook to get an idea of the content you will cover as you complete your study of the human body.

Step 2: Complete the chart. In each box, write the name of a body system discussed in the mini-lesson.

Step 3: Draw one of the body systems in the body outline.

Step 4: Cut out the title and glue it to the front cover of your notebook.

Step 5: Cut out the chart. Apply glue to the back and attach it below the title.

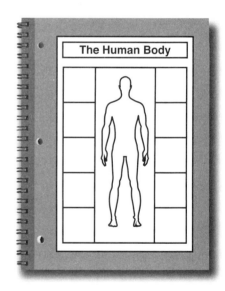

Mini-Lesson

The Human Body

The human body is a wonderful machine. To understand how the machine works, you need to understand how your body is organized. The body is made up of cells, tissues, and organs. These parts, working together, are called a system. Your body has a number of systems that keep it working properly.

The systems of the body include the circulatory, lymphatic, skeletal, excretory, muscular, endocrine, digestive, nervous, respiratory, and reproductive. It is important to understand the purpose of each body system and how the systems work together to maintain a stable condition inside your body.

Systems of the Human Body

- **Skeletal System** provides the framework for your body.

- **Muscular System** partners with the skeletal system to help the body move.

- **Digestive System** helps turn food into a form that can be used by the body.

- **Excretory System** expels waste from the body.

- **Respiratory System** brings oxygen into the body and gets rid of carbon dioxide.

- **Circulatory System** transports materials through the body.

- **Lymphatic and Immune Systems** utilize the same organs. The lymphatic system moves fluid from the tissues to the circulatory system. The immune system guards the human body against diseases.

- **Nervous System** carries messages throughout the body.

- **Endocrine System** is made up of glands that produce and release hormones that regulate the activity of cells or organs.

- **Reproductive System** includes the organs that work together for the purpose of reproduction.

The Human Body

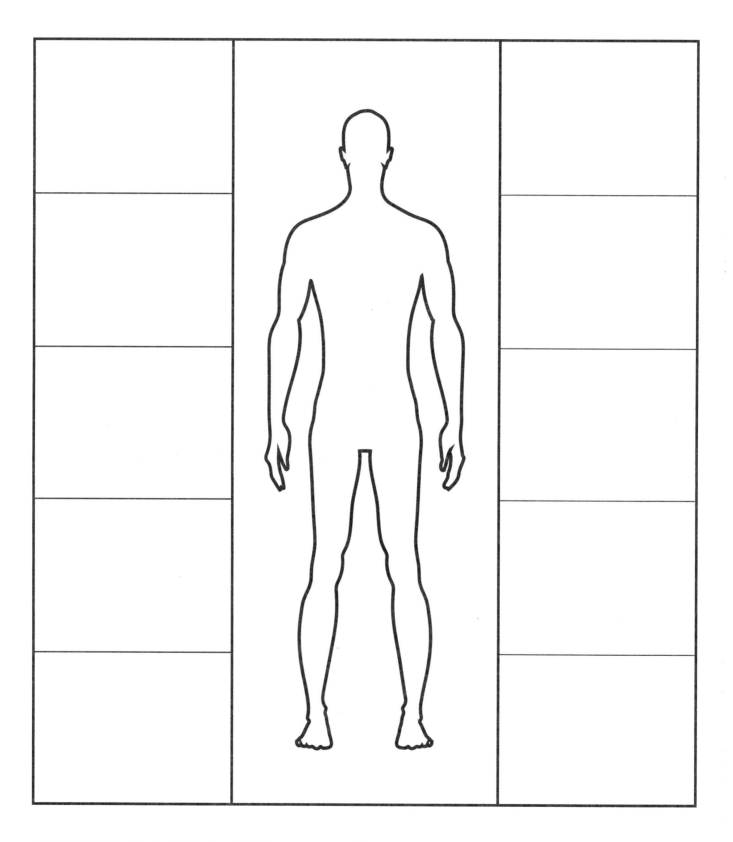

Student Instructions: The Human Cell

Materials Needed

Glue, scissors, colored pencils

How to Create a Right-hand Interactive Notebook Page

Read the Mini-Lesson page. Then cut out the box and attach it to the right-hand page of your interactive notebook. Use what you have learned to create the left-hand page.

How to Create Your Left-hand Interactive Notebook Page

Complete the following steps to create the left-hand page of your interactive notebook. Use lots of color.

Step 1: Cut out the title and glue it to the top of the notebook page.

Step 2: Cut out the *Human Cell Diagram*. Apply glue to the back and attach the diagram below the title.

Step 3: Cut out the eight definition pieces and glue each piece in the correct box on the diagram.

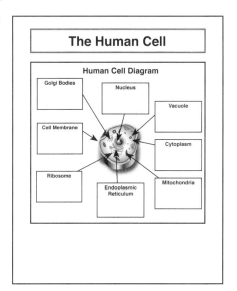

Demonstrate and Reflect on What You Have Learned

Observe a cheek cell. Add a drop of iodine to a slide. Use the blunt end of a toothpick to gently scrape the inside lining of your cheek. Place the blunt end of the toothpick on the slide and mix it with the iodine. Place a cover slip over the solution. View the slide under a microscope. Record your observations in your interactive notebook.

Mini-Lesson

The Human Cell

The human body is made up of trillions of tiny cells. **Cells** are living units and are able to make more cells like themselves. They are responsible for keeping humans alive. All new cells can only come from existing cells.

Cells make up your blood, bone, muscle, nerves, and skin. There are about 200 different types of cells in the human body. Each cell type has a specific job located in different regions of the body.

The human cell has four basic parts.

- **Nucleus:** This dense, ball-shaped part is located near the center of the cell and controls the cell's activities and the cell's ability to reproduce. Structures called chromosomes are found here. These structures are made of segments of DNA called genes. Genes determine the inheritance of a particular trait. For example, blue or brown eyes, blond or black hair.
- **Nuclear membrane:** This surrounds and protects the nucleus.
- **Cytoplasm:** This gel-like fluid is made of water, salts, and other materials and takes up most of the space inside a cell.
- **Cell membrane:** This thin, flexible membrane surrounds the entire cell. It keeps the cell together and controls the movement of materials into and out of the cell.

The human cell has a variety of small structures inside the cytoplasm called organelles; each perform a job for the cell.

- **Vacuoles:** These liquid-filled organelles store food, water, and waste.
- **Endoplasmic reticulum:** These tube-shaped organelles produce and move proteins and lipids within the cell. They also serve as an internal delivery system for the cell.
- **Ribosomes:** Some of these organelles are attached to the endoplasmic reticulum; others are just in the cytoplasm. They receive directions from the DNA to make proteins.
- **Golgi bodies:** These organelles help package and distribute proteins outside the cell.
- **Mitochondria:** These organelles use oxygen to transform the energy in food molecules to make and release energy. They are the "powerhouses" of the cell.

The Human Cell

Human Cell Diagram

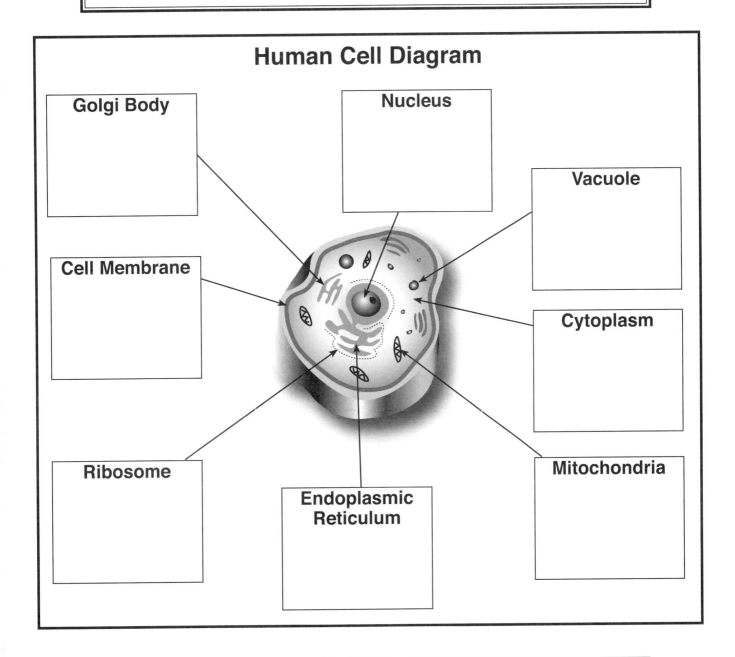

Golgi Body

Nucleus

Vacuole

Cell Membrane

Cytoplasm

Ribosome

Mitochondria

Endoplasmic Reticulum

packages and distributes protein outside the cell	control center for the cell	gel-like fluid that contains organelles	encloses the cell
makes protein for the cell	makes energy for the cell	transportation system for the cell	stores food, water, and waste for the cell

Student Instructions: Cells, Tissues, Organs, and Systems

Materials Needed

Glue, scissors, colored pencils

How to Create a Right-hand Interactive Notebook Page

Read the Mini-Lesson page. Then cut out the page and attach it to the right-hand page of your interactive notebook. Use what you have learned to create the left-hand page.

How to Create a Left-hand Interactive Notebook Page

Complete the following steps to create the left-hand page of your interactive notebook. Use lots of color.

Step 1: Cut out the title and glue it to the top of the notebook page.

Step 2: Cut out the *Organization of Body Systems* chart. Apply glue to the back and attach the chart below the title.

Step 3: Fill in the boxes in the chart. Write the name and function of each level of the system.

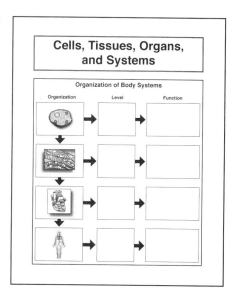

Demonstrate and Reflect on What You Have Learned

Think about what you have learned about the organization of the human body systems. In your interactive notebook, explain the difference between a cell, tissue, and an organ.

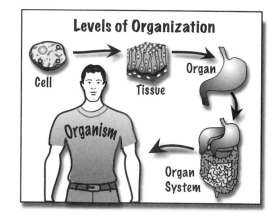

Mini-Lesson

Cells, Tissues, Organs, and Systems

Cells, **tissues**, and **organs** are the levels in the organization of a human body system. Each part of the system works together to perform a specific function.

Cells are the smallest units of life. They make up all living things and carry out the activities that keep a living thing alive. The human body is made of trillions of very tiny cells. Cells have different shapes, sizes, and color. Sometimes cells work alone. An example of this is when red blood cells carry oxygen to other body cells. Sometimes they work with other cells; a group of cells that work together to perform the same job is called a tissue.

Tissues are made of a group of similar cells that work together to do the same job. An individual cell does its part to keep the tissue alive. The human body is made up of several types of tissue. For example, muscle cells join together to make muscle tissue. The cells in muscle tissue work together to make the body move. There are four kinds of tissue: muscle tissue, epithelial (covering) tissue, connective tissue, and nerve tissue. Tissues that are similar and do the same job are organized into a larger part of the body called an organ.

Organs are structures that are made up of two or more tissues that work together to do a specific job. Each organ does a specific job to make all the human body systems run smoothly. For example, the heart is an organ made up of blood tissue (liquid connective tissue), muscle tissue, and nerve tissue. The heart muscle contracts, making the heart pump blood. The nerve tissue receives messages that tell the heart how fast to beat or pump the blood. The human body has many organs: kidneys, stomach, and brain to name a few. A group of organs that work together to carry out a certain job makes up an organ system.

A **system** is made up of all the organs that work together to do the same job. For example, the circulatory system of the human body includes the heart, veins, and capillaries. The body has systems that work together to keep it alive. There are ten main systems: skeletal, muscular, digestive, excretory, respiratory, circulatory, lymphatic, nervous, endocrine, and reproductive.

Interesting Facts
- Motor neuron cells are the longest cells in the human body. Running from the lower spinal cord to the big toe, they can measure up to 4.5 feet (1.37 meters) long.
- Red blood cells are created in the bone marrow of your bones. They are responsible for carrying oxygen throughout the body.

Cells, Tissues, Organs, and Systems

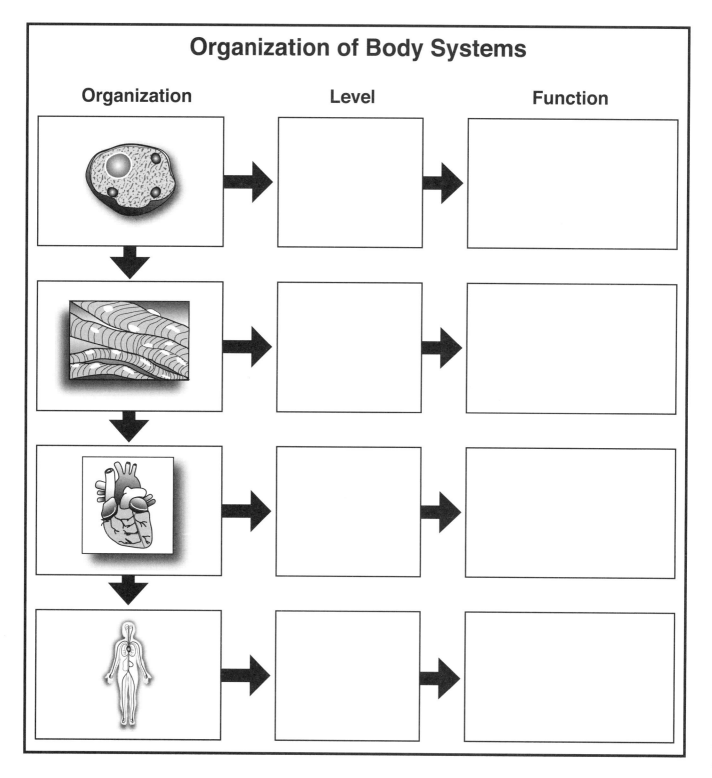

Student Instructions: Skeletal System

Materials Needed

Glue, scissors, colored pencils

How to Create a Right-hand Interactive Notebook Page

Read the Mini-Lesson page. Then cut out the page and attach it to the right-hand page of your interactive notebook. Use what you have learned to create the left-hand page.

How to Create a Left-hand Interactive Notebook Page

Complete the following steps to create the left-hand page of your interactive notebook. Use lots of color.

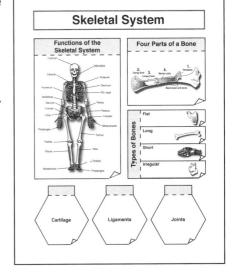

Step 1: Cut out the title and glue it to the top of the notebook page.

Step 2: Cut out the *Functions of the Skeletal System* flap piece. Apply glue to the back of the gray tab and attach the flap piece below the title. Under the flap, describe the functions of the skeletal system.

Step 3: Cut out the *Four Parts of a Bone* flap piece. Apply glue to the back of the gray tab and attach the flap piece below the title. Under the flap, describe the function of each part of the bone.

Step 4: Cut out the *Types of Bones* flap book. Cut along the solid lines to create four flaps. Apply glue to the back of the gray tab and attach the flap book below the *Four Parts of a Bone* flap piece. Under each flap, describe the function of the bone.

Step 5: Cut out the three hexagonal flap pieces. Apply glue to the back of the gray tabs and attach the pieces at the bottom of the page. Under each flap, write the function of that part of the skeletal system.

Demonstrate and Reflect on What You Have Learned

Think about what you have learned. Design and construct a 3-D bone model; label the parts. Use online or print resources to help you with the project. Share the model with your classmates.

Mini-Lesson

Skeletal System

The **skeletal system** provides the framework for the human body. The skeletal system performs five jobs.

1. **Supports and shapes:** The skeletal system shows the size and shape of the body and provides support for the many parts inside the body.
2. **Protects the organs inside the body:** Parts of the skeletal system protect vital organs such as the brain, heart, and lungs.
3. **Works with the muscular system to move the parts of the body:** Together the two systems allow the body to move. Muscles are attached to bones in the skeletal system. Contracting or relaxing those muscles lets the bones move up, down, forward, and backward.
4. **Make blood cells:** The skeletal system makes blood cells.
5. **Store minerals:** The skeletal system stores the extra minerals the body may not need after eating in the bones until the body needs them.

The skeletal system is made up of 206 individual bones. The bone consists of the following parts.

1. **Periosteum:** membrane that covers the surface of the bone, containing small blood vessels that bring nutrients to the bone.
2. **Spongy bone:** lightweight bone with small, open spaces like sponge found at the ends of longer bones.
3. **Compact bone:** a hard layer of bone under the periosteum that contains blood vessels, bone cells, and deposits of protein, calcium, and phosphorus.
4. **Bone marrow:** found in the center of long bones and in the spaces of spongy bone where blood cells are made.

Bones are classified into four groups. Each type of bone has a particular shape and function.

1. **Flat bones:** flat, often curved; protect internal organs such as the brain and heart.
2. **Long bones:** long, tubular, enlarged ends; provide support and protection, serve as levers.
3. **Short bones:** like irregular cube shapes; support weight, allow small movements
4. **Irregular bones:** all other shapes; support for the body and protecting the spinal cord

The skeletal system is held together by cartilage, ligaments, and joints.

- **Cartilage:** The hard flexible tissue that first forms the skeletal system. As the body ages, most of the cartilage is replaced by bone. It also helps reduce bone-on-bone friction at the joints.
- **Ligaments:** The strong, stretchy connective tissue that holds bones together.
- **Joints:** The places in the skeleton where bones meet.

Skeletal System

Functions of the Skeletal System

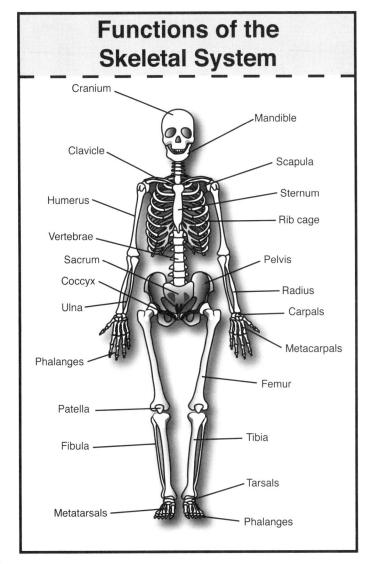

Cranium
Mandible
Clavicle
Scapula
Humerus
Sternum
Rib cage
Vertebrae
Sacrum
Pelvis
Coccyx
Radius
Ulna
Carpals
Metacarpals
Phalanges
Femur
Patella
Fibula
Tibia
Tarsals
Metatarsals
Phalanges

Four Parts of a Bone

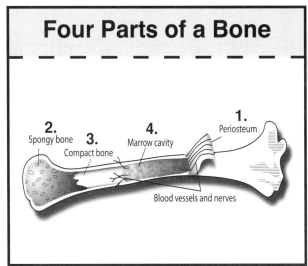

2. Spongy bone
3. Compact bone
4. Marrow cavity
1. Periosteum
Blood vessels and nerves

Types of Bones

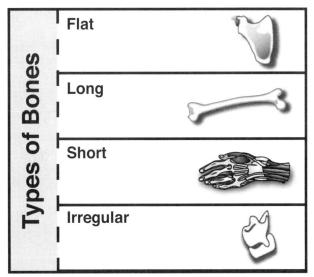

Flat

Long

Short

Irregular

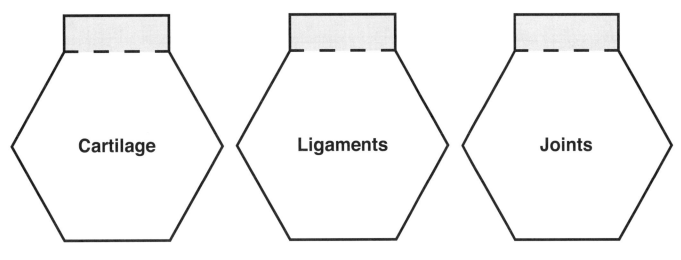

Cartilage

Ligaments

Joints

Student Instructions: Joints of the Human Body

Materials Needed

Glue, scissors, colored pencils

How to Create a Right-hand Interactive Notebook Page

Read the Mini-Lesson page. Then cut out the page and attach it to the right-hand page of your interactive notebook. Use what you have learned to create the left-hand page.

How to Create a Left-hand Interactive Notebook Page

Complete the following steps to create the left-hand page of your interactive notebook. Use lots of color.

Step 1: Cut out the title and glue it to the top of the notebook page.

Step 2: Cut out the *Kinds of Joints* flap book. Cut on the solid lines to create five flaps. Apply glue to the back of the gray tab and attach the flap book below the title.

Step 3: Under each flap, write a brief description of the joint.

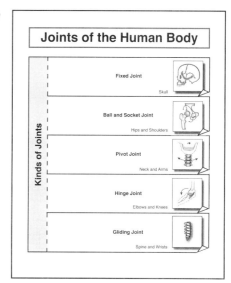

Demonstrate and Reflect on What You Have Learned

Create a chart like the one to the right in your interactive notebook. Think about which joints you use to perform the different activities listed and then complete the chart. If an activity uses more than one kind of joint, explain which part of the action uses which joint.

Activity	Kinds of Joints Used
throwing a ball	
bending over to pick up something	
playing the piano	

Joints of the Human Body

The skeletal system contains joints. A **joint** is a part of the body where two or more bones meet. With over 200 bones in the human skeleton, bones meet in many places. Joints help the bones give shape and support to the body, provide protection, and work with the muscular system to help the body move. In fact, helping the body with movement is the major function of a joint. The human body has five different kinds of joints.

Kinds of Joints

- **Fixed Joint:** This kind of joint allows little or no movement. The fixed joints of the human skull help protect the brain.
- **Ball and Socket:** This joint allows circular movement. They let the bones swing in almost any direction and are found in the shoulder and hips of the human body.
- **Pivot Joint:** This kind of joint allows bones to rotate around each other. One bone is stationary, another rotates around it. They are found in neck and elbows.
- **Hinge Joint:** This joint works like the opening and closing of a door. The movement is in one direction and is found in the knees, elbows, fingers, and toes.
- **Gliding Joint:** This kind of joint allows movement back and forth and also from side to side; the bones slide over each other. They are found in the wrists and spine.

At each joint, the bones have to be far enough apart not to rub against each other but still be able to stay in place. Cartilage and ligaments help the joints perform effectively.

Holding Bones and Joints Together

- **Cartilage:** This hard flexible tissue is also thick and smooth and often covers the ends of bones at joints. It works like a built-in shock absorber in a joint. The slippery cushion allows bones to slide and reduces friction against pressure.
- **Ligaments:** These strong, stretchy bands of connective tissue hold the bones of many joints together. When too much pressure is put on a joint, ligaments may tear; this is called a sprain and occurs most often at the knees, ankles, and fingers.

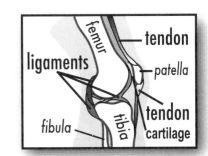

- **Tendons:** These bands of dense, tough, inelastic, white, fibrous tissue, connect muscles with a bone or another part.

Joints of the Human Body

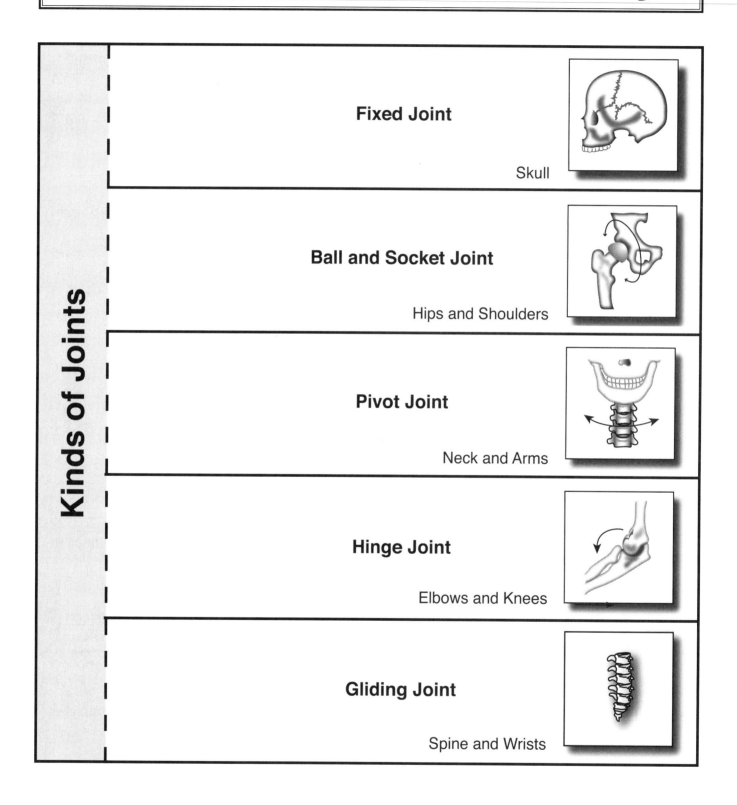

Kinds of Joints

Fixed Joint

Skull

Ball and Socket Joint

Hips and Shoulders

Pivot Joint

Neck and Arms

Hinge Joint

Elbows and Knees

Gliding Joint

Spine and Wrists

Student Instructions: Muscular System

Materials Needed

Glue, scissors, colored pencils

How to Create a Right-hand Interactive Notebook Page

Read the Mini-Lesson page. Then cut out the page and attach it to the right-hand page of your interactive notebook. Use what you have learned to create the left-hand page.

How to Create a Left-hand Interactive Notebook Page

Complete the following steps to create the left-hand page of your interactive notebook. Use lots of color.

Step 1: Cut out the title and glue it to the top of the notebook page.

Step 2: Cut out the *What is the Difference?* flap book. Apply glue to the back of the gray center section and attach it below the title. Under each flap, write the definition.

Step 3: Cut out the puzzle pieces. Match each kind of muscle with its two description pieces. Glue the matching pieces at the bottom of the page to create three complete rows.

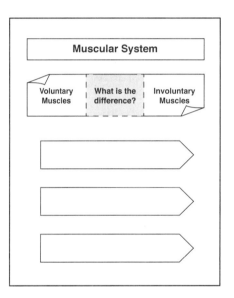

Demonstrate and Reflect on What You Have Learned

Think about the voluntary and involuntary muscles in the human body. Why is it a good thing that not all of the muscles are voluntary? Explain your answer in your interactive notebook.

Mini-Lesson

The Muscular System

The **muscular system** controls the movement of the human body. The bones and joints of the skeletal system work with the muscular system to make the body move. Some muscles work without thinking; others are controlled by thinking. There are three kinds of muscle.

A **muscle** is an organ that contracts and expands, creating movement. There are over 600 muscles in the human body. Muscles not only help you move, but they also help give your body shape and produce heat in your body. Every minute of the day and night, there is always some muscle moving in your body. There are two main groups of muscles: voluntary muscles and involuntary muscles.

- **Voluntary Muscles:** These are muscles that you control consciously (in other words, you think about when and how to move them). They work with the skeletal system to perform various activities. For example, if you think about playing basketball, you tell the brain, and the body does the rest.
- **Involuntary Muscles:** These muscles work automatically (you don't have to think about them). For example, the heart pumps blood throughout your body day and night without you telling it to.

There are three types of muscle tissue in your body.

- **Skeletal Muscles:** These muscles move bones. They are attached to the bones with **tendons**, thick bands of tissue. They are the voluntary muscles (that you choose to move). They are the most common type of muscle in your body. They control your posture and your body movements. Under a microscope, they look striated or striped. They contract and relax quickly. Blood vessels bring them oxygen and food, and nerves connect to them to bring them the messages from your brain about when and how to move.

- **Smooth Muscles:** This type of muscle is found in the walls of many of your organs, such as your intestines and blood vessels, and in your skin. They are involuntary (work automatically). They contract and relax slowly. They are not striated. They are thin muscles. These muscles are responsible for pushing materials through passages in your body. For example, they push food through your digestive system.

- **Cardiac Muscles:** This type of muscle is found only in the heart. It is involuntary (works on its own). Like skeletal muscles, it has striations, but the cells weave together a little differently. The job of these muscles is to pump blood throughout your body. This type of muscle contracts nonstop all day and night for your whole life.

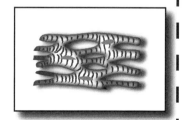

Muscular System

Voluntary Muscles	What is the difference?	Involuntary Muscles

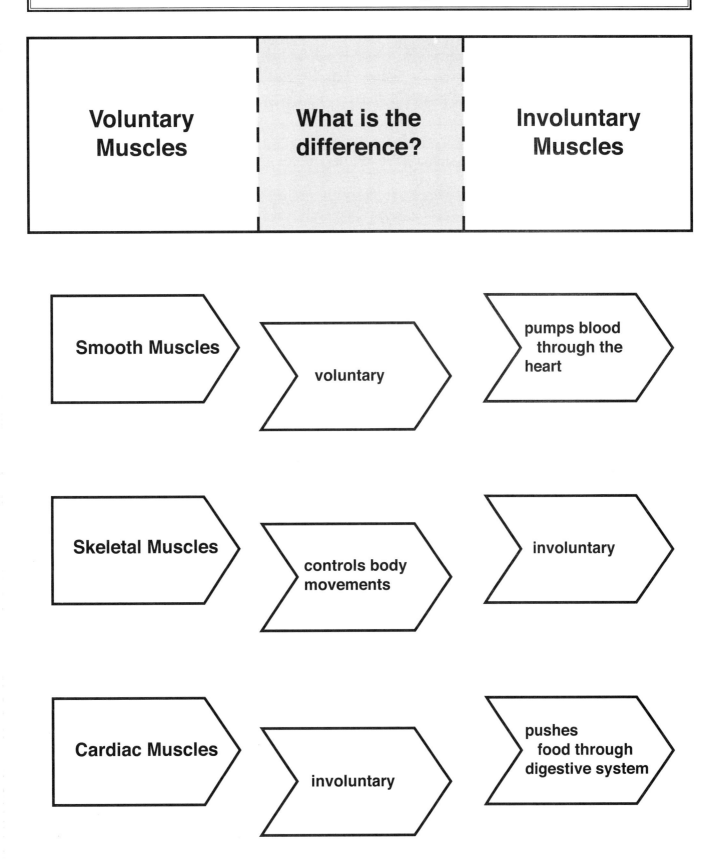

Smooth Muscles

voluntary

pumps blood through the heart

Skeletal Muscles

controls body movements

involuntary

Cardiac Muscles

involuntary

pushes food through digestive system

Student Instructions: Digestive System

Materials Needed

Glue, scissors, colored pencils

How to Create a Right-hand Interactive Notebook Page

Read the Mini-Lesson page. Then cut out the page and attach it to the right-hand page of your interactive notebook. Use what you have learned to create the left-hand page.

How to Create a Left-hand Interactive Notebook Page

Complete the following steps to create the left-hand page of your interactive notebook. Use lots of color.

Step 1: Cut out the title and glue it to the top of the notebook page.

Step 2: Cut out the *Connected Organs of the Digestive Tract* flap book. Cut on the solid lines to create five flaps. Apply glue to the back of the gray section and attach the flap book below the title. Write the name of the organ on each flap. Under the flap, explain the function of the organ.

Step 3: Cut out the *What is the Difference?* flap book. Apply glue to the back of the gray center section and attach the flap book to the bottom of the page. Under each flap, describe the kind of digestion.

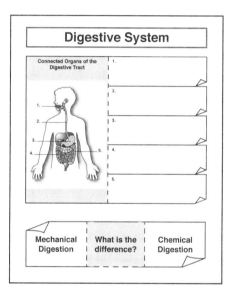

Demonstrate and Reflect on What You Have Learned

There has been a lot of discussion in recent years regarding eating disorders found in middle-school students such as anorexia, bulimia, and binge eating. Research the disorders and write a summary of each in your interactive notebook.

Mini-Lesson

Digestive System

Digestion is the process used to break down food into substances the body can use. There are two kinds of digestion.

- **Mechanical Digestion:** This digestion breaks food into smaller pieces.
- **Chemical Digestion:** This digestion changes the food chemically using special proteins called enzymes to change the food eaten into smaller molecules that can be taken in by cells.

The **digestive system** includes all of the organs responsible for digestion. This includes the five connected organs that make up the digestive tract and several other organs (not directly connected to the digestive tract) that help them as they do their jobs.

Organs of the Digestive Tract

- **Mouth:** The teeth grind food into smaller pieces. Saliva begins digesting starches, breaking them down into sugars and softening food before swallowing.
- **Esophagus:** This organ is a muscular tube in the throat that squeezes the food into the stomach using waves of contracting muscle called **peristalsis**.
- **Stomach:** This bag-like muscular organ is where food is further digested. Chewed up food is mixed and churned with gastric juices (enzymes, mucus, and hydrochloric acid) until it is adequately broken down. This liquid food mixture is now called **chyme**.
- **Small Intestine:** This organ is the longest part of the digestive system. The chyme leaves the stomach and passes through three sections of the small intestine. Digested food is absorbed by tiny fingerlike structures called villi that line the walls of the small intestine; then nutrients are carried to cells in the body.
- **Large Intestine:** This organ, also called the **colon**, holds the materials that cannot be digested. It absorbs the remaining water trapped in the food waste. The solid remaining is called **feces**. Feces is stored in the rectum until it is full and then expelled from the body through the **anus**.

Other Organs Aiding the Digestive System

- **Salivary Glands:** located under the jaw and tongue and in front of each ear; they produce saliva, or spit, that begins the chemical digestion of food.
- **Pancreas:** located behind the stomach; the enzymes made here break down carbohydrates and proteins.
- **Liver:** located on top of the stomach, it makes bile, a liquid stored in the **gallbladder** (located under the liver). **Bile** breaks up large fat molecules in the small intestine.

Digestive System

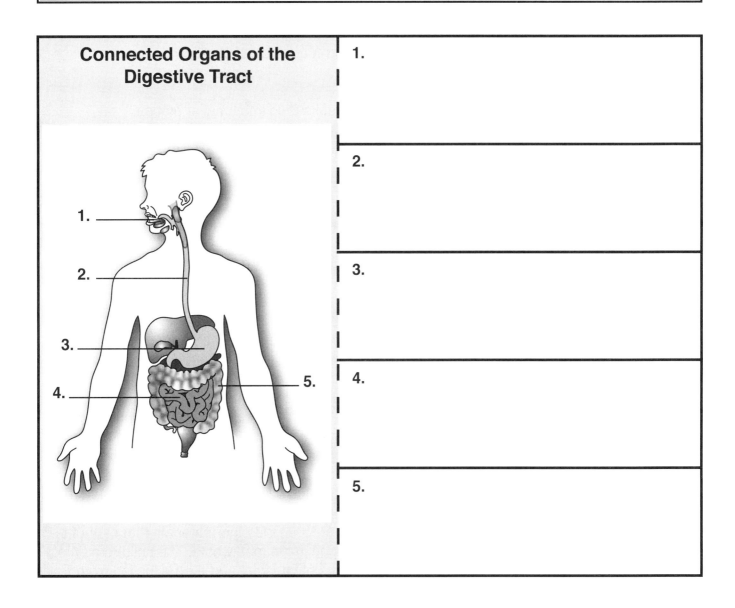

Connected Organs of the Digestive Tract

1.

2.

3.

4.

5.

Mechanical Digestion	What is the difference?	Chemical Digestion

Student Instructions: Excretory System

Materials Needed

Glue, scissors, colored pencils

How to Create a Right-hand Interactive Notebook Page

Read the Mini-Lesson page. Then cut out the page and attach it to the right-hand page of your interactive notebook. Use what you have learned to create the left-hand page.

How to Create a Left-hand Interactive Notebook Page

Complete the following steps to create the left-hand page of your interactive notebook. Use lots of color.

Step 1: Cut out the title and glue it to the top of the notebook page.

Step 2: Fill in the blanks on the *Job of the Excretory System* flap book. Cut out the flap book. Cut on the solid lines to create four flaps. Apply glue to the back of the gray center section. Attach the flap book below the title.

Step 3: Under each flap, describe how the system or organ removes waste from the body.

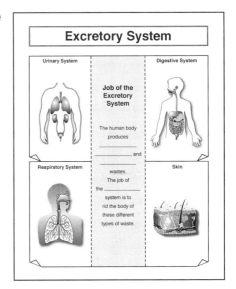

Demonstrate and Reflect on What You Have Learned

Think about how the body eliminates wastes. Demonstrate the removal of water through your skin. You will need a plastic bag, rubber band, and a stopwatch. Place the plastic bag over one hand and secure it with a rubber band around the wrist. Leave the bag on for five minutes. Record your observations in your interactive notebook.

Now demonstrate the removal of water through your respiratory system. You will need a small hand mirror. Hold the mirror close to your mouth and exhale. Record your observations in your interactive notebook.

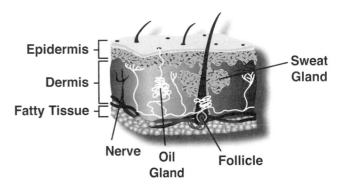

Mini-Lesson

Excretory System

The job of the **excretory system** is ridding the body of wastes produced by the activity of cells. The human body produces solid, liquid, and gaseous wastes. Each kind of waste is removed by a different part of the body.

The excretory system works with other body systems and the skin to remove wastes from the body.

- **Urinary System:** This system works with the excretory system to remove liquid waste, **urine**, that has been filtered in the body's bloodstream. The system consists of four main parts.
  1. **Kidneys:** The human body has two of these bean-shaped organs that are located on the back wall of the abdomen at waist level. All blood passes through tiny filters called **nephrons**. Liquid waste carried in blood collects in these filters and forms urine.
  2. **Ureters:** These long tubes move the urine from the kidneys to the bladder.
  3. **Bladder:** This elastic storage holds the urine from the kidneys.
  4. **Urethra:** This tube carries urine from the bladder and out the body during urination.
- **Respiratory System:** This system works with the excretory system to remove gaseous wastes. As waste gases from the blood move to the lungs, they diffuse into the alveoli in the lungs and are expelled when exhaling.
- **Digestive System:** This system works with the excretory system to remove solid wastes from the body. Remains of the food we eat move into the large intestine where excess water is removed; the rest (feces) is stored in the rectum until it is full. Then the feces moves out of the body through the anus.
- **Skin:** The body's largest organ, the skin works with the excretory system to remove liquids. The top layer of skin contains millions of sweat glands. These sweat glands release wastes in the form of sweat, excess water, salt, and **urea** (a protein).

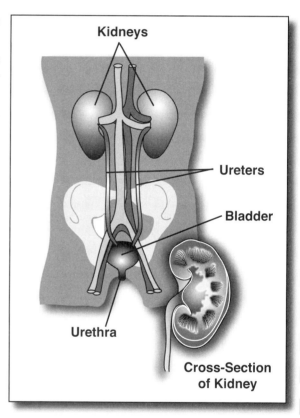

Kidneys

Ureters

Bladder

Urethra

Cross-Section of Kidney

Excretory System

Urinary System

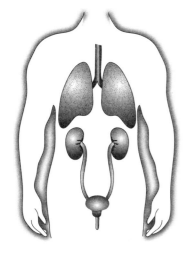

Job of the Excretory System

The human body produces

_____,

_____, and

_____

wastes.

The job of

the _____

system is to

rid the body of

these different

types of waste.

Digestive System

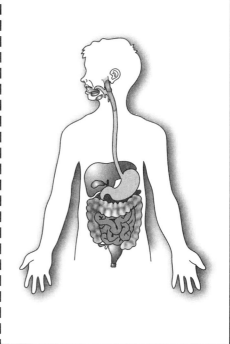

Respiratory System

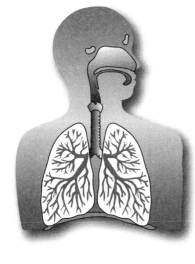

Skin

Student Instructions: Respiratory System

Materials Needed

Glue, scissors, colored pencils

How to Create a Right-hand Interactive Notebook Page

Read the Mini-Lesson page. Then cut out the page and attach it to the right-hand page of your interactive notebook. Use what you have learned to create the left-hand page.

How to Create a Left-hand Interactive Notebook Page

Complete the following steps to create the left-hand page of your interactive notebook. Use lots of color.

Step 1: Cut out the title and glue it to the top of the notebook page.

Step 2: Cut out the *Respiratory Tract* flap book. Cut on the solid lines to create five flaps. Apply glue to the back of the diagram section and attach the flap book below the title. Under each flap, write the name of the structure or organ being described.

Step 3: Cut out the *Breathing vs. Respiration* flap book. Cut on the solid line to create two flaps. Apply glue to the back of the gray tab and attach the flap book at the bottom of the page. Under each flap, describe the process.

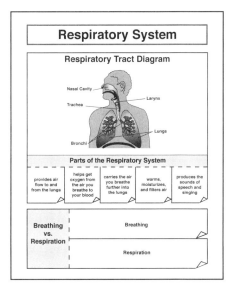

Demonstrate and Reflect on What You Have Learned

Measure your resting and running breathing rates. Count the number of times you exhale in one minute. Record the results in your interactive notebook. Repeat the procedure two more times. Find the average for the three trials. Record the average. Repeat the procedure after running in place for one minute. Compare the results of the resting breathing rate and the exercising breathing rate.

Mini-Lesson

Respiratory System

The job of the **respiratory system** is to get oxygen into the body and remove carbon dioxide that the cells produce as a gaseous waste. Breathing and respiration are the key elements of the respiratory system.

- **Breathing:** This is the mechanical process of taking air into and out of the body. As fresh air is brought into the lungs, it brings oxygen to the circulatory system and cells. Stale air is removed from the lungs, expelling the carbon dioxide wastes produced by the cells.
- **Respiration:** This is a chemical process that involves using oxygen to get energy from food. Respiration takes place within the cells. The digestive system makes glucose in the cells from digested food. Oxygen combines with glucose in a chemical reaction that releases energy. Carbon dioxide is a waste product of respiration that is carried back to the lungs and expelled when exhaling.

The respiratory system is made up of structures and organs that allow oxygen to move into the body and remove waste gases out of the body. In the respiratory tract, air follows a certain pathway in and out of the lungs.

- **Nasal Cavity:** Air enters through two holes in the nose called **nostrils** or through the mouth and enters the nasal cavity. The function of the nasal cavity is to warm, moisturize, and filter air entering the body before it reaches the lungs.
- **Pharynx:** This is also called the throat. It is a tube that connects to the trachea; **cilia** line the pharynx and filter out particles that weren't caught before.
- **Epiglottis:** This is a flap of tissue at the end of the pharynx. It seals the windpipe, or trachea, when you are eating.
- **Larynx:** This segment of the respiratory tract is also called the "voice box," as the vocal cords are attached to this airway. Using air from the lungs, it produces the sounds of speech and singing.
- **Trachea:** This tube is also called the windpipe. It provides air flow to and from the lungs.
- **Lungs:** These two organs are cone-shaped and are an elaborate latticework of tubes. The main function of the lungs is to help oxygen from the air we breathe enter the red cells in the blood. The lungs consist of the bronchi, the bronchioles, and the alveoli. The trachea branches into the **bronchi**, which are two tubes that carry air into each lung. Each tube is called a bronchus. Each bronchus branches off further into thousands of smaller and smaller tubes called **bronchioles**. The **alveoli** are clusters of tiny air sacs at the end of the smallest bronchioles. Oxygen passes from the alveoli into the blood vessels; at the same time, carbon dioxide carried in the blood moves from the tiny blood vessels into the alveoli. Carbon dioxide moves up through the respiratory system and is exhaled from the body.
- **Diaphragm:** This is a large curved muscle located below the rib cage. It expands and contracts the rib cage, causing the body to inhale or exhale.

Respiratory System

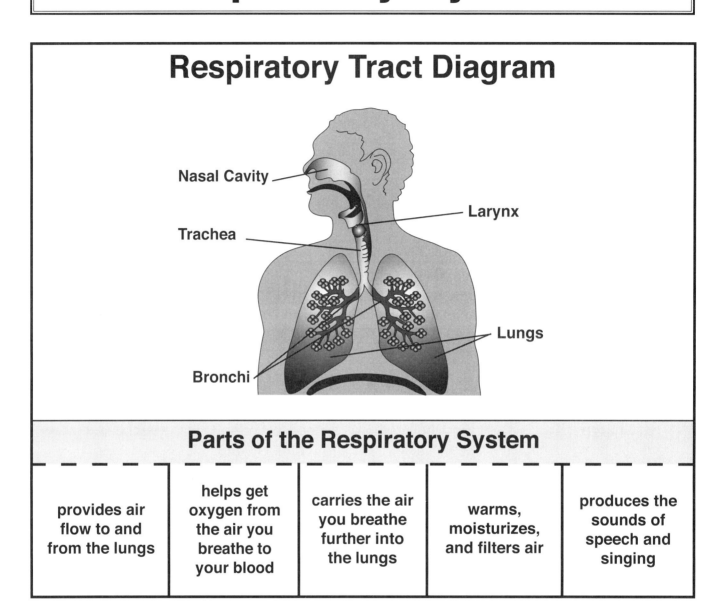

Respiratory Tract Diagram

Nasal Cavity

Larynx

Trachea

Lungs

Bronchi

Parts of the Respiratory System

provides air flow to and from the lungs	helps get oxygen from the air you breathe to your blood	carries the air you breathe further into the lungs	warms, moisturizes, and filters air	produces the sounds of speech and singing

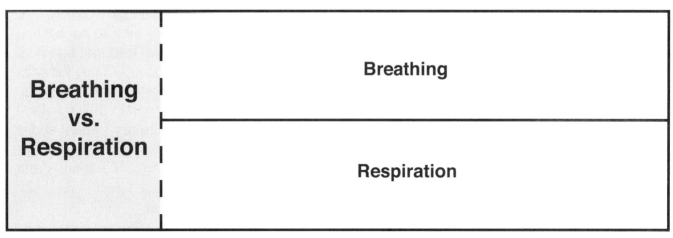

Breathing vs. Respiration

Breathing

Respiration

Student Instructions: Circulatory System

Materials Needed

Glue, scissors, colored pencils

How to Create a Right-hand Interactive Notebook Page

Read the Mini-Lesson page. Then cut out the page and attach it to the right-hand page of your interactive notebook. Use what you have learned to create the left-hand page.

How to Create a Left-hand Interactive Notebook Page

Complete the following steps to create the left-hand page of your interactive notebook. Use lots of color.

Step 1: Cut out the title and glue it to the top of the notebook page.

Step 2: Cut out the *Parts of the Heart* flap book. Cut on the solid lines to create four flaps. Apply glue to the back of the heart diagram section and attach the flap book below the title. Under each flap, answer the question.

Step 3: Cut out the *Three Sections of the Circulatory System* flap book. Cut on the solid lines to create three flaps. Apply glue to the back of the gray tab and attach the flap book at the bottom of the page. Under each flap, describe the function of the section.

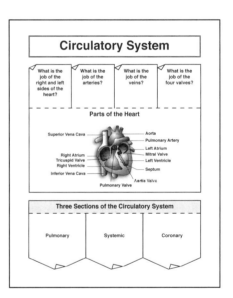

Demonstrate and Reflect on What You Have Learned

Think about what you have learned. In your interactive notebook, write a creative "help wanted" ad for the circulatory system. Provide a good description of the job requirements, hours, and expectations.

Mini-Lesson

Circulatory System

The **circulatory system** is responsible for transporting needed substances throughout the body and carrying away wastes. The system is made up of the body's heart, blood, arteries, veins, and blood vessels called capillaries.

The fist-sized **heart**, located in the middle of the chest, is the main organ of the circulatory system. It has a number of important parts.

- **Four chambers:** The two upper chambers are called the **right atrium** and the **left atrium**. The two lower chambers are called the **right ventricle** and the **left ventricle**. The right side of the heart receives blood from the body and pumps it to the lungs. The left side receives blood from the lungs and pumps it out to the body.
- **Four valves:** These are located between the chambers and act like doors that only open one way to make sure the blood goes in or out. The **tricuspid valve** opens from the right atrium into the right ventricle. The **pulmonary valve** opens from the right ventricle letting blood flow into the pulmonary artery leading out of the heart. The **mitral valve** opens from the left atrium to the left ventricle. The **aortic valve** lets blood flow from the left ventricle out of the heart through the aorta.
- **Arteries:** These large blood vessels carry blood away from the heart. The **aorta** is the main artery leaving the left ventricle. The main artery leaving the right ventricle is the **pulmonary artery**.
- **Veins:** These blood vessels carry blood to the heart.
- **Capillaries:** These tiny blood vessels connect arteries and veins. Nutrients and oxygen in the blood are exchanged between the capillaries and cells.

Scientists have divided circulation into three sections. The beating of the heart controls the blood flow through each section.

- **Pulmonary circulation:** The circulation of blood as it moves through the heart, to the lungs, where it picks up oxygen, and travels back to the heart.
- **Systemic circulation:** The circulation of oxygen-rich blood as it travels to all the body tissues and organs.
- **Coronary circulation:** The circulation of blood to and from the tissues of the heart.

Blood is a tissue made up of cells and cell parts that are carried in a liquid. It is made up of four parts.

- **Red blood cells:** These disc-shaped cells contain a protein called hemoglobin and deliver oxygen and remove carbon dioxide.
- **White blood cells:** These cells are varied in shape and size and help the body fight disease.
- **Platelets:** These irregularly shaped cell pieces help the blood clot if you have an injury.
- **Plasma:** This is the pale yellow liquid (mostly water) part of blood. It carries dissolved foods to blood cells.

Circulatory System

What is the job of the right and left sides of the heart?	What is the job of the arteries?	What is the job of the veins?	What is the job of the four valves?

Parts of the Heart

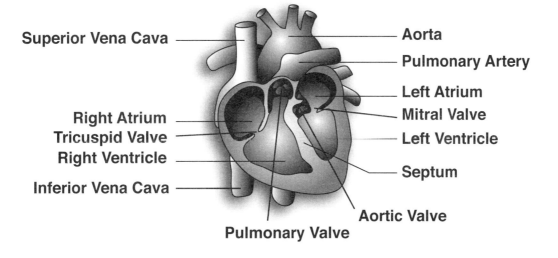

Superior Vena Cava

Right Atrium
Tricuspid Valve
Right Ventricle
Inferior Vena Cava

Pulmonary Valve

Aorta
Pulmonary Artery
Left Atrium
Mitral Valve
Left Ventricle
Septum

Aortic Valve

Three Sections of the Circulatory System

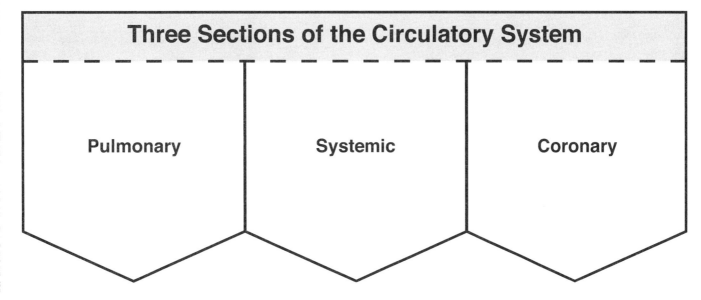

Pulmonary   Systemic   Coronary

Student Instructions: Lymphatic and Immune Systems

Materials Needed

Glue, scissors, colored pencils

How to Create a Right-hand Interactive Notebook Page

Read the Mini-Lesson page. Then cut out the page and attach it to the right-hand page of your interactive notebook. Use what you have learned to create the left-hand page.

How to Create a Left-hand Interactive Notebook Page

Complete the following steps to create the left-hand page of your interactive notebook. Use lots of color.

Step 1: Cut out the title and glue it to the top of the notebook page.

Step 2: Fill in the blanks on the *Functions of the Two Systems* piece. Cut out the piece. Apply glue to the back and attach it below the title.

Step 3: Cut out the *Parts of the Lymphatic and Immune Systems* diagram piece. Apply glue to the back and attach the piece at the bottom of the page. Write the name of each part of the system on the correct numbered line.

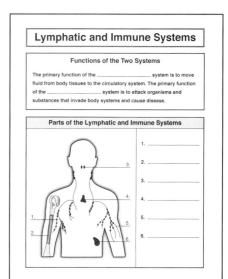

Demonstrate and Reflect on What You Have Learned

Think about what you have learned. In your interactive notebook, explain the connection between the lymphatic system and the immune system.

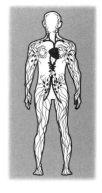

Mini-Lesson

Lymphatic and Immune Systems

The lymphatic system works closely with the immune system. The organs of the lymphatic system and the immune system are the same. The primary function of the **lymphatic system** is to move fluid from body tissues to the circulatory system. The main job of the **immune system** is to attack organisms and substances that invade body systems and cause disease.

Lymphatic System

The **lymphatic system** is another system that carries fluids in your body and uses vessels and capillaries. In between your cells is a tissue fluid that contains dissolved substances and some of the water that comes out of your blood. This extra fluid is collected by the lymphatic system and then returned to the blood through **lymph capillaries** and **vessels** that carry it to large veins near the heart.

Lymph nodes are bean-shaped structures through which the lymph passes before it returns to the blood. Here is where microorganisms and foreign materials are filtered out. Major lymph nodes include:

- **Tonsils** (at the back of your mouth): There are two of these located on both sides of the back of the throat. The main function is to trap bacteria and viruses that you may breathe in. These lumps of tissue may become infected and swollen. When this happens, a type of white blood cell called **lymphocytes**, produced in the bone marrow, surrounds and destroys the bacteria or virus.
- **Thymus** (behind your sternum): This small butterfly-shaped gland lies at the base of the neck. It promotes the development of lymphocytes that are sent to other organs in the lymphatic system.
- **Spleen** (behind the upper left part of the stomach): This is the largest lymph node; it is located behind the upper left part of the stomach. It filters blood and breaks down damaged red blood cells.

Immune System

The **immune system** protects the body against diseases caused by microscopic invaders called **pathogens**. These bacteria, viruses, and fungi are all around us. Generally, the body's skin, tears, and saliva work to keep the pathogens from getting into the body, but sometimes they do make it through.

Once inside the body, pathogens are attacked by lymphocytes. These white blood cells either attack the pathogens directly or produce **antibodies**. Antibodies bind to pathogens and help destroy them. Each antibody is designed to attack only one type of pathogen. Therefore, each type of pathogen requires its own type of antibody. White blood cells that make antibodies remember pathogens they have fought before. So if a pathogen comes back, the cells can quickly make more antibodies to fight it. Pathogens in the blood are removed at lymph node locations.

Lymphatic and Immune Systems

Functions of the Two Systems

The primary function of the _____ system is to move fluid from body tissues to the circulatory system. The primary function of the _____ system is to attack organisms and substances that invade body systems and cause disease.

Parts of the Lymphatic and Immune Systems

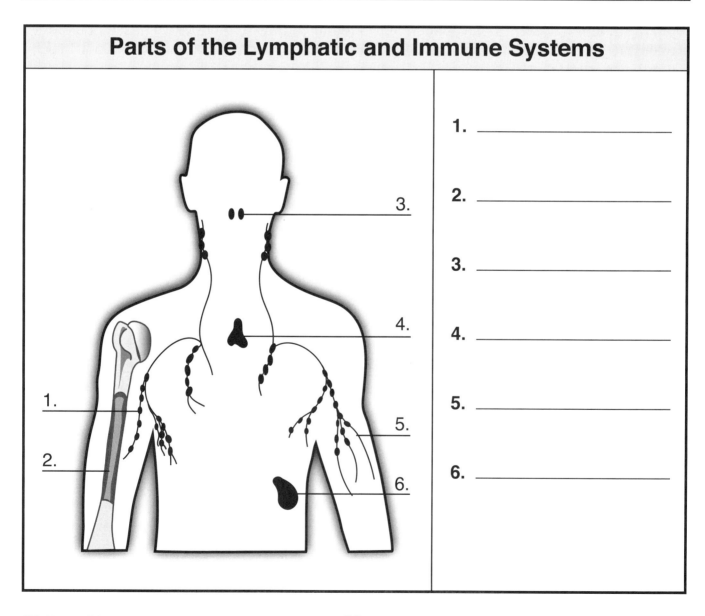

1. _____

2. _____

3. _____

4. _____

5. _____

6. _____

Student Instructions: Nervous System

Materials Needed

Glue, scissors, colored pencils

How to Create a Right-hand Interactive Notebook Page

Read the Mini-Lesson page. Then cut out the page and attach it to the right-hand page of your interactive notebook. Use what you have learned to create the left-hand page.

How to Create a Left-hand Interactive Notebook Page

Complete the following steps to create the left-hand page of your interactive notebook. Use lots of color.

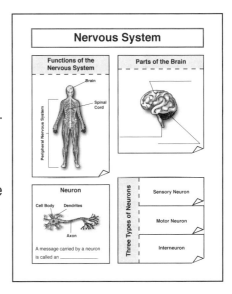

Step 1: Cut out the title and glue it to the top of the notebook page.

Step 2: Cut out the *Functions of the Nervous System* flap piece. Apply glue to the back of the gray tab and attach the flap piece below the title. Under the flap, write the five functions of the nervous system.

Step 3: Cut out the *Parts of the Brain* flap piece. Label the three parts of the brain. Apply glue to the back of the gray tab and attach the flap piece below the title. Under the flap, write the functions of each part of the brain.

Step 4: Fill in the blank on the *Neuron* piece. Cut out the piece. Apply glue to the back and attach the piece to the bottom of the page.

Step 5: Cut out the *Three Types of Neurons* flap book. Cut on the solid lines to create three flaps. Apply glue to the back of the gray tab and attach the flap book at the bottom of the page. Under each flap, write the function of the neuron.

Demonstrate and Reflect on What You Have Learned

Think about the three main parts of the brain. Which part would you use for each of the following activities? Write the answers in your interactive notebook.

1. Smelling a fire burning 2. Running and dribbling a basketball 3. Breathing

Nervous System

The **nervous system** is the message center for the body. It receives, interprets, and responds to stimuli from inside and outside the body.

Five Functions of the Nervous System
- maintains **homeostasis** (balance) in your body. It coordinates all body systems.
- responds to stimuli in the environment around you. Helps you understand and respond to anything you see, hear, smell, taste, touch, feel, or think.
- maintains your consciousness.
- responsible for your learning and your memory.
- controls the automated parts of body systems, such as the beating of your heart.

Two Parts of the Nervous System
- The **central nervous system** includes your brain and spinal cord.
- The **peripheral nervous system** includes all the other nerves in your body.

Three Parts of the Brain
- **Cerebrum:** This part of the brain is where your thinking and learning take place. It interprets the information gathered by your senses. The cerebrum is divided into two sides called hemispheres. The right hemisphere of the brain controls the left side of your body and is generally the creative side. The left hemisphere of the brain controls the right side of your body and generally is the logical, reasoning side.
- **Cerebellum:** This part of the brain lies behind and under the cerebrum. It helps you maintain your balance and coordination.
- **Brain Stem:** This part of the brain lies at the base of your brain. It connects the brain to the spinal cord. It coordinates the involuntary muscle movements for functions such as the beating of your heart and your breathing.

Neurons are Specialized Cells of the Nervous System
A message carried by a neuron is called an **impulse.** The main parts of a neuron are:
- **cell body:** main part of the cell that includes the nucleus.
- **dendrites:** receive incoming messages.
- **axon:** carries outgoing messages.

Three Types of Neurons
- **Sensory neurons:** receive information and send impulses to the spinal cord and the brain.
- **Motor neurons:** relay impulses from the brain or spinal cord to parts of the body.
- **Interneurons:** relay impulses between the sensory and motor neurons.

Nervous System

Functions of the Nervous System

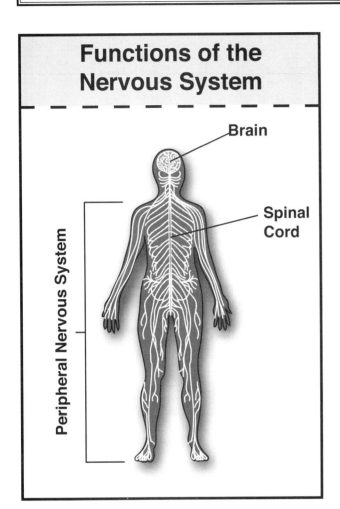

Brain

Spinal Cord

Peripheral Nervous System

Parts of the Brain

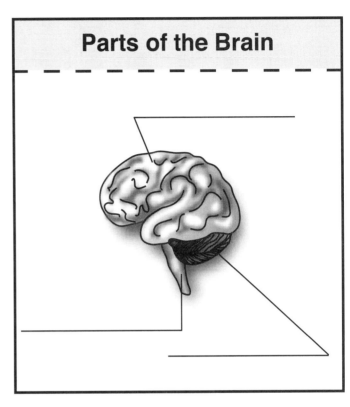

Neuron

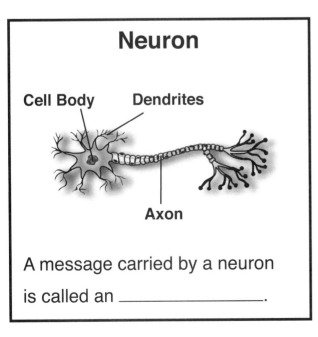

Cell Body

Dendrites

Axon

A message carried by a neuron is called an _____.

Three Types of Neurons

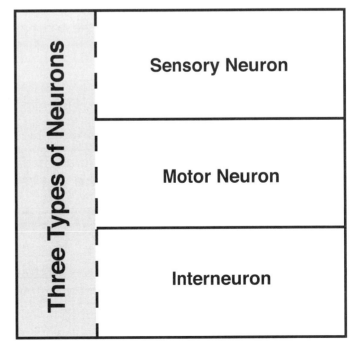

Sensory Neuron

Motor Neuron

Interneuron

Student Instructions: The Five Senses

Materials Needed

Glue, scissors, colored pencils

How to Create a Right-hand Interactive Notebook Page

Read the Mini-Lesson page. Then cut out the page and attach it to the right-hand page of your interactive notebook. Use what you have learned to create the left-hand page.

How to Create a Left-hand Interactive Notebook Page

Complete the following steps to create the left-hand page of your interactive notebook. Use lots of color.

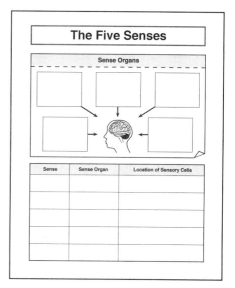

Step 1: Cut out the title and glue it to the top of the notebook page.

Step 2: Draw one of the sense organs in each blank box on the *Sense Organs* flap piece. Cut out the flap piece. Apply glue to the back of the gray tab and attach the piece below the title. Under the flap, explain how the nervous system and the five sense organs work together to process information taken in from the environment.

Step 3: Complete the chart. Cut out the chart and apply glue to the back. Attach it at the bottom of the page.

Demonstrate and Reflect on What You Have Learned

In your interactive notebook, draw a diagram of each sense organ and label the parts. Use online or print resources to help you with the project.

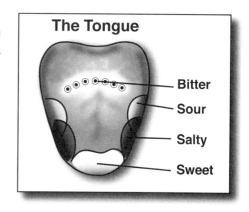

Mini-Lesson

The Five Senses

The **nervous system** receives and processes information about your environment. Much of this information is taken into your body through five sense organs: eyes, ears, tongue, nose, and skin. Each organ has special cells, called **sensory cells**, that receive the information and translate it into signals the nervous system can use. The nervous system responds to the information and then transmits it to your brain. Your brain interprets these signals, making you aware of your surroundings.

The **eyes** are the sense organs for sight. Light waves enter your eyes and are bent first by the **cornea** followed by the **lens**. The rays of light are then directed onto the sensory cells located in the retina, which sits at the very back of your eye. The energy from the light waves stimulates impulses in the **rods** and **cones**. These impulses travel to the **optic nerve**, which carries them to the brain where the image is interpreted.

The **ears** are the sense organ for hearing. The ear has three parts: the outer ear, the middle ear, and the inner ear. The sensory cells are located inside the inner ear. Sound enters the outer ear. It travels in a tube called the **auditory canal**. This leads to the **eardrum**. A membrane in the middle ear vibrates along with three tiny bones in the middle ear: the **hammer**, **anvil**, and **stirrup**. The middle ear sends the vibration to the inner ear also called the **cochlea**. The cochlea transforms the sound into nerve impulses that travel to the brain.

The **tongue** is the sense organ for taste. The surface of the tongue is covered with thousands of sensory cells called **taste buds**. In order to taste, the food must be dissolved in the saliva (a digestive liquid secreted by glands in your mouth). As the food dissolves, sensory cells signal the taste center in the brain. The brain interprets the taste as salty, sweet, sour, or bitter.

The **nose** is the sense organ for smell. The odor of food comes from molecules that food gives off into the air. The sensory cells called **olfactory cells** line the **nasal cavity**. They are covered with mucous glands, which help keep them moist. Molecules of food in the air travel into the nasal cavity and dissolve in the mucus. The olfactory cells are stimulated and send an impulse to the brain, where the odor is identified if it is one you have smelled before. If it is a new smell, a new odor memory will be created.

The **skin** is the sense organ for touch. Sensory cells are found just below the skin's surface. These cells react to touch, pain, temperature, and pressure. They transmit signals through the spinal cord to the brain, the brain then responds to the sensation.

The Five Senses

Sense Organs

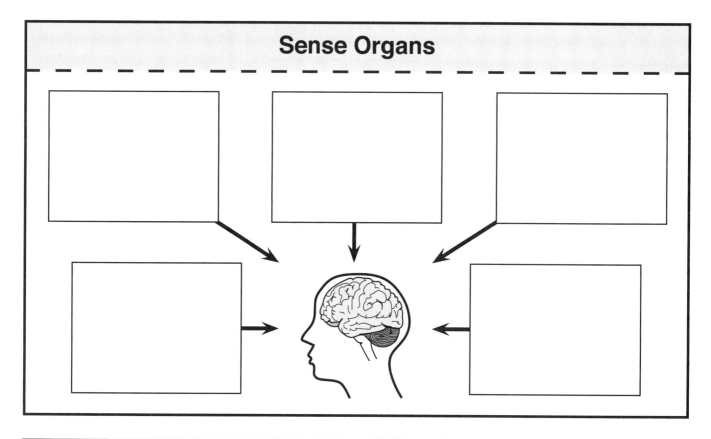

Sense	Sense Organ	Location of Sensory Cells

Student Instructions: Endocrine System

Materials Needed

Glue, scissors, colored pencils

How to Create a Right-hand Interactive Notebook Page

Read the Mini-Lesson page. Then cut out the page and attach it to the right-hand page of your interactive notebook. Use what you have learned to create the left-hand page.

How to Create a Left-hand Interactive Notebook Page

Complete the following steps to create the left-hand page of your interactive notebook. Use lots of color.

Step 1: Cut out the title and glue it to the top of the notebook page.

Step 2: Cut out the *Endocrine Glands* flap piece. Apply glue to the back of the gray tab and attach the piece below the title. Under the flap, write the functions of the endocrine system.

Step 3: Complete the chart. Cut out the chart and apply glue to the back. Attach it at the bottom of the page.

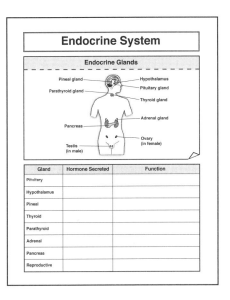

Demonstrate and Reflect on What You Have Learned

Think about what you have learned. In your interactive notebook, explain the similarity between the endocrine system and the nervous system.

Systems

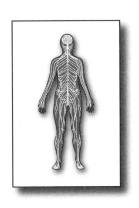
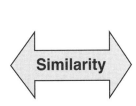
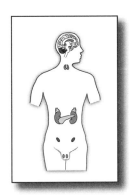

Endocrine System

The **endocrine system** uses chemicals called **hormones** to control other body systems. The hormones are produced by glands and released directly into the bloodstream. The circulatory system then carries the chemicals throughout the body. When the chemicals arrive at the target tissues, they start to do their work.

The endocrine system does not control your body all by itself. It has some help from another system called the nervous system. The nervous system uses signals sent along nerves to tell other parts of the body what to do. The endocrine system uses chemicals, released into the blood, to tell other systems what to do. The nervous system controls the body quickly, and the results are over with quickly. The endocrine system, however, may take a long time to react, and the effects may last for days, weeks, months, or even years.

There are nine major **glands** of the endocrine system that release hormones to keep conditions inside your body stable.

- **Pituitary:** This small gland is about the size of a marble. It is found at the base of the cerebrum. It is the master gland. It releases hormones that control the other glands. One hormone made by the pituitary is the **human growth hormone (HGH)**. It controls the growth of muscles, bones, and organs. The pituitary also controls the reproductive glands.
- **Hypothalamus:** This collection of cells located in the lower central part of the brain produces hormones that tell the pituitary gland to produce more or less of certain hormones. These hormones include **anti-diuretic hormone**, **oxytocin**, and **somatostatin**.
- **Pineal:** The pineal gland is located in the middle of the brain. It produces **melatonin**, a hormone that helps the body regulate when it is time to sleep or wake.
- **Thyroid:** This is a butterfly-shaped gland in the throat. It secretes the hormone thyroxine. This controls your body's metabolism (the rate at which your body uses up the food you eat).
- **Parathyroids:** These four pea-sized glands secrete the hormone **parathormone**. It controls the levels of calcium and phosphate in your blood. Calcium helps keep your teeth and bones healthy. Phosphate helps keep the right pH level in your blood.
- **Adrenal glands:** These glands sit on top of the kidneys. The outer layer makes more than 30 hormones. They control the amount of salt in your blood. The inner layer makes **adrenaline**—the "fight or flight" hormone, which gives you sudden bursts of strength and energy. In times of sudden fear, pain, or anger, your body makes adrenaline.
- **Pancreas:** This gland is found behind your stomach. It releases several hormones, including **insulin**, which helps control the blood sugar level in your body.
- **Reproductive glands**
    - Female: The **ovaries** are located in the pelvic region and produce the hormones **estrogen** and **progesterone**, which affect female traits.
    - Male: The **testes** are located in the scrotum and produce the hormone **testosterone**, which affects male traits.

Endocrine System

Endocrine Glands

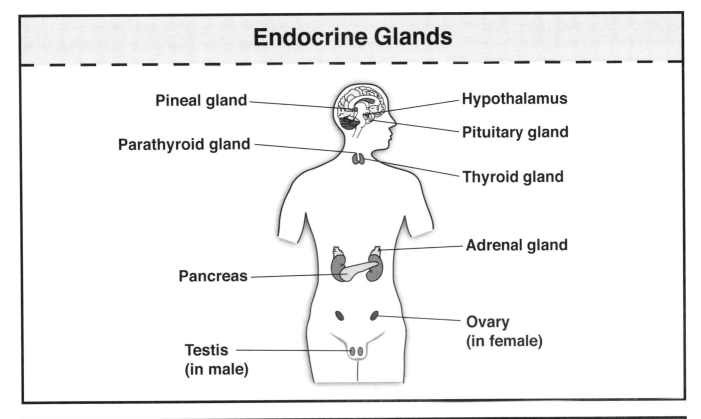

Pineal gland

Hypothalamus

Pituitary gland

Parathyroid gland

Thyroid gland

Adrenal gland

Pancreas

Ovary
(in female)

Testis
(in male)

Gland	Hormone Secreted	Function
Pituitary		
Hypothalamus		
Pineal		
Thyroid		
Parathyroid		
Adrenal		
Pancreas		
Reproductive		

Student Instructions: Sexual Reproduction

Materials Needed

Glue, scissors, colored pencils

How to Create a Right-hand Interactive Notebook Page

Read the Mini-Lesson page. Then cut out the page and attach it to the right-hand page of your interactive notebook. Use what you have learned to create the left-hand page.

How to Create a Left-hand Interactive Notebook Page

Complete the following steps to create the left-hand page of your interactive notebook. Use lots of color.

Step 1: Cut out the title and glue it to the top of the notebook page.

Step 2: Cut out the four *Question* flap pieces. Apply glue to the back of the gray tabs and attach each flap piece below the title.

Step 3: Under each flap, answer the question.

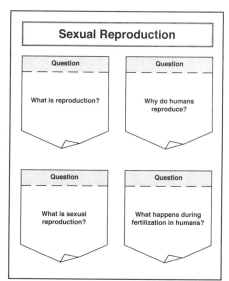

Demonstrate and Reflect on What You Have Learned

In your interactive notebook, draw a diagram illustrating the very first stage of life, which starts with the union of sperm cell and the egg cell forming the zygote cell.

Sperm Cell + Egg Cell = Human Zygote

Sexual Reproduction

Reproduction

Reproduction is a biological process by which living things make more of their own kind. When living things reproduce, many **traits**, or characteristics, of the parents are passed to their offspring.

Humans Reproduce

Reproduction is a natural instinct that humans are born with. It is essential for our survival as a species to produce offspring. Without offspring, the human race would eventually become endangered or even extinct.

Sexual Reproduction

Sexual reproduction is a process in which cells from two different parents unite to form a new cell that develops into a new human being. The individual receives genetic material from both parents.

Sexual Reproduction in Humans

In humans, the process of reproduction involves the combination of genetic information from the parents. The body of each parent produces special cells called **sex cells**, or reproductive cells. Both cells are needed to make a new human being. A **sperm cell** is the sex cell produced in the **testes** of the male parent. An **egg cell**, or ovum, is the sex cell produced in the **ovaries** of the female parent.

During sexual reproduction, a sperm cell unites with an egg cell in a process called **fertilization**. The fertilized cell, called a **zygote**, contains genetic information from both parents. The zygote cell begins to divide to make more cells. In about 40 weeks, a fully developed baby is formed. This new human being has some traits of both parents.

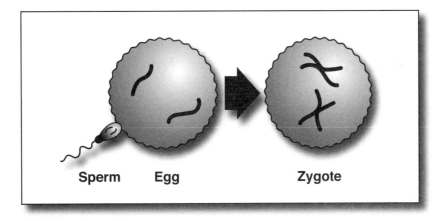

Sperm   Egg   Zygote

Sexual Reproduction

Question

What is reproduction?

Question

Why do humans reproduce?

Question

What is sexual reproduction?

Question

What happens during fertilization in humans?

Student Instructions: Male and Female Reproductive Systems

Materials Needed

Glue, scissors, colored pencils

How to Create a Right-hand Interactive Notebook Page

Read the Mini-Lesson page. Then cut out the page and attach it to the right-hand page of your interactive notebook. Use what you have learned to create the left-hand page.

How to Create a Left-hand Interactive Notebook Page

Complete the following steps to create the left-hand page of your interactive notebook. Use lots of color.

Step 1: Cut out the title and glue it to the top of the notebook page.

Step 2: Cut out the two pockets. Fold back the gray tabs on the dotted lines. Apply glue to the tabs and attach each pocket below the title.

Step 3: Cut apart the sentence strips. Place each strip in the correct pocket.

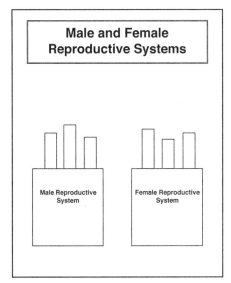

Demonstrate and Reflect on What You Have Learned

List the organs of the male and female reproductive systems in your interactive notebook. After the name of each organ, explain its function.

Mini-Lesson

Male and Female Reproductive Systems

Human reproduction involves both the male and female reproductive systems. Both systems produce **sex cells**, or reproductive cells. During human reproduction, two sex cells, a **sperm cell** produced in the male reproductive system and an **egg cell** produced in the female reproductive system, unite in the female reproductive system to create a new individual.

Puberty

The stage in the development of humans when the sex organs of both males and females become mature and capable of reproduction is called **puberty**. Puberty begins during adolescence. For girls, adolescence occurs between the ages of about 11 and 14. In boys, puberty occurs between the ages of about 13 and 16.

Male Reproductive System
- The organs of the male reproductive system include sperm ducts, urethra, testes, and penis.
- The organs are located on the outside of the body and within the pelvis.
- When **sperm** is released, it travels up from the **testes** through **sperm ducts** to the **urethra**.
- Sperm leaves the body through the urethra, which travels through the **penis**.

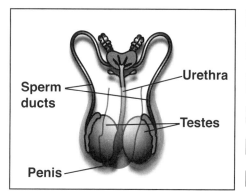

Female Reproductive System
- The organs of the female reproductive system include ovaries, fallopian tubes, uterus, and vagina.
- The organs are located within the body.
- During **ovulation**, an egg leaves one of the two **ovaries** and travels through a **fallopian tube** toward the **uterus**.
- Each month, blood begins to thicken the lining of the uterus to prepare for a fertilized egg. One of two things can happen at this stage.
  1. A sperm deposited in the **vagina** travels up the fallopian tube and finds the egg. The egg is fertilized by the sperm cell as it travels from the fallopian tube to the uterus. The egg attaches to the wall of the uterus and begins to develop.
  2. No fertilized egg attaches to the wall of the uterus. As a result, the blood lining begins breaking down. The blood then leaves the body through the vagina in what is known as **menstruation**.

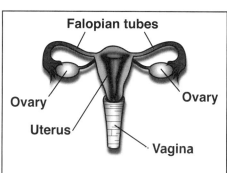

Male and Female Reproductive Systems

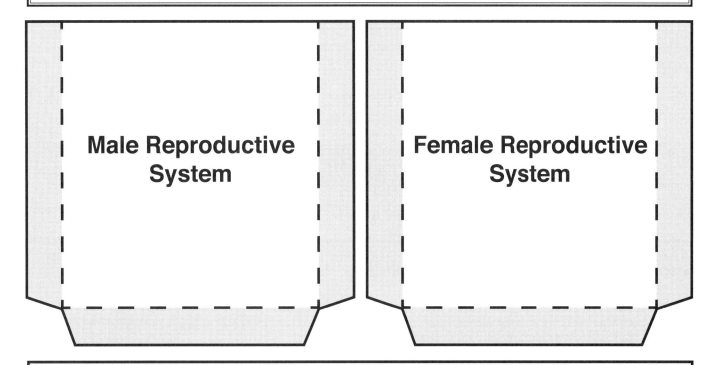

Male Reproductive System

Female Reproductive System

Reproductive organs are located on the outside of the body and within the pelvis.

Reproductive system that produces the egg cell.

Reproductive organs are located within the body.

Reproductive organs include the sperm ducts, urethra, testes, and penis.

Reproductive system that produces the sperm cell.

Reproductive organs include the ovaries, fallopian tubes, uterus, and vagina.

Student Instructions: Genetics

Materials Needed

Glue, scissors, colored pencils

How to Create a Right-hand Interactive Notebook Page

Read the Mini-Lesson page. Then cut out the page and attach it to the right-hand page of your interactive notebook. Use what you have learned to create the left-hand page.

How to Create a Left-hand Interactive Notebook Page

Complete the following steps to create the left-hand page of your interactive notebook. Use lots of color.

Step 1: Cut out the title and glue it to the top of the notebook page.

Step 2: Cut out the *Relationships Among the Cell, Chromosomes, DNA, and Genes* flap piece. Apply glue to the back of the gray tab and attach the flap piece below the title. Under the flap, write a brief summary of the relationship.

Step 3: Cut out the *Sex Chromosomes* flap book. Cut on the solid line to create two flaps. Apply glue to the back of the gray tab and attach the flap book at the bottom of the page. Draw the correct chromosome on the front of each flap. Under each flap, describe the chromosome.

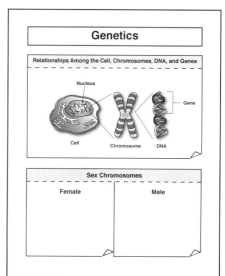

Demonstrate and Reflect on What You Have Learned

Design a three-dimensional model that illustrates the basic structure of both the female and male sex chromosomes. Use online or print resources if you need help.

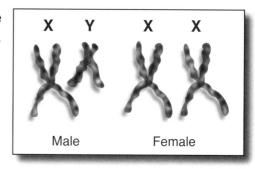

Mini-Lesson

Genetics

When humans reproduce, characteristics, or **traits**, of the parents, such as eye and hair color, are passed on to their children. Scientists studied cells for many years before they discovered how this was possible. By the end of the nineteenth century, scientists had learned the secret code of **heredity**, or passing physical and character traits from one generation to another. They found that traits are controlled by genes made up of DNA located on the chromosomes found in the nucleus of the human cell.

The Cell, Chromosomes, DNA, and Genes
- Inside every **cell** is a genetic code or chemical blueprint for how a human being looks and functions.
- The **nucleus** is the most important structure inside a cell. It can be thought of as the control center of the cell.
- **Chromosomes** are tiny rod-shaped strands of genetic material found inside the nucleus of a cell. Humans have 23 pairs of chromosomes in each cell. One set of chromosomes for each pair comes from the mother, and the other set of chromosomes comes from the father.
- Chromosomes are made from molecules of **DNA** (deoxyribonucleic acid).
- A **gene** is a short section of the DNA ladder. The order of the molecules on the ladder in that section form a **genetic code**, instructions for creating specific proteins for the development of a trait passed from parent to offspring. Humans have thousands of different genes.

Sex Chromosomes
The sex of a person is determined by a pair of chromosomes known as the **sex chromosomes**. There are two types: the X chromosome and Y chromosome. Females have two X chromosomes (XX). Males have one X and one Y chromosome (XY).

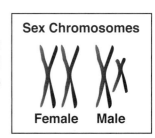

Sex Chromosomes

Female   Male

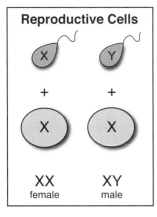

Reproductive Cells

XX
female

XY
male

Reproductive Cells
The female reproductive cell, or **egg cell**, has one X chromosome. The male reproductive cell, or **sperm cell**, has either an X or Y chromosome. When the egg and sperm cells unite, it forms the first cell of a new human being. The cell will grow and develop into either a female or male individual.
- When a sperm with an X chromosome joins with an egg, the fertilized egg will contain chromosomes XX. It will develop into a female.
- When a sperm with a Y chromosome joins with an egg, the fertilized egg will contain chromosomes XY. It will develop into a male.

Genetics

Relationships Among the Cell, Chromosomes, DNA, and Genes

Nucleus

Gene

Cell

Chromosome

DNA

Sex Chromosomes

Female	Male

Student Instructions: Heredity

Materials Needed

Glue, scissors, colored pencils

How to Create a Right-hand Interactive Notebook Page

Read the Mini-Lesson page. Then cut out the page and attach it to the right-hand page of your interactive notebook. Use what you have learned to create the left-hand page.

How to Create a Left-hand Interactive Notebook Page

Complete the following steps to create the left-hand page of your interactive notebook. Use lots of color.

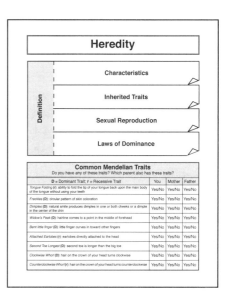

Step 1: Cut out the title and glue it to the top of the notebook page.

Step 2: Cut out the *Definition* flap book. Cut on the solid lines to create four flaps. Apply glue to the back of the gray tab and attach the flap book below the title. Under each flap, write the definition.

Step 3: Complete the *Common Mendelian Traits* chart. Cut out the chart and apply glue to the back. Attach it at the bottom of the page.

Demonstrate and Reflect on What You Have Learned

In your interactive notebook, describe five traits you inherited from your parents.

Freckles are an inherited trait.

Mini-Lesson

Heredity

The **characteristics** of all living things are called **traits**. Every living thing is a collection of **inherited traits**, characteristics passed down to an individual by the parents. The passing of traits from parents to offspring is called **heredity**. These traits are controlled by genes made up of DNA and chromosomes located in the nucleus of cells.

Reproduction that requires two parents is called **sexual reproduction**. Each individual that is produced is unique. The parents only pass some of their traits to their child. Each child gets different traits from each of its parents. The child will not be exactly like their parents or other children produced by their parents.

Many inherited traits are easy to identify such as eye color, hair color, and height. Traits that control genetic health conditions can also be inherited from the parents. These traits can increase the risk of the child developing conditions including diabetes, asthma, and cancer.

Gregor Mendel was the first person to describe how traits are inherited. His studies of inherited traits led to the **Laws of Dominance**, principles of genetics. He noticed that genes always came in pairs. A trait may be **dominant** (stronger), and that trait will show up in the individual. If a trait is **recessive** (weaker), it will not show up unless the individual inherits two recessive genes.

Straight Little Finger   **Bent Little Finger**

Inherited Trait

A straight or bent
little finger was inherited
from your parents.

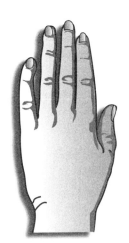

Heredity

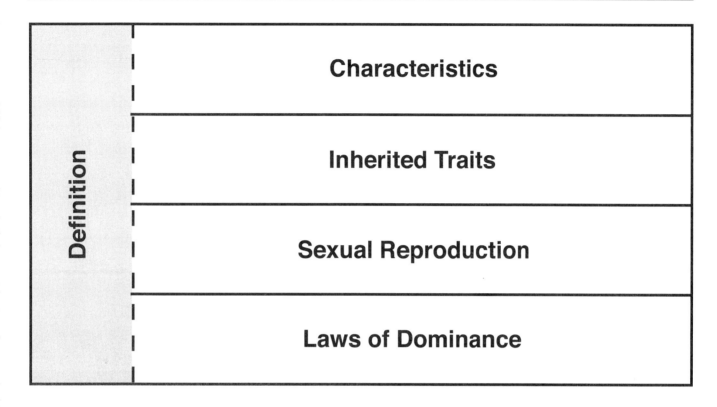

Definition	Characteristics
	Inherited Traits
	Sexual Reproduction
	Laws of Dominance

Common Mendelian Traits

Do you have any of these traits? Which parent also has these traits?

D = Dominant Trait; r = Recessive Trait	You	Mother	Father
Tongue Folding (r): ability to fold the tip of your tongue back upon the main body of the tongue without using your teeth	Yes/No	Yes/No	Yes/No
Freckles (D): circular pattern of skin coloration	Yes/No	Yes/No	Yes/No
Dimples (D): natural smile produces dimples in one or both cheeks or a dimple in the center of the chin	Yes/No	Yes/No	Yes/No
Widow's Peak (D): hairline comes to a point in the middle of forehead	Yes/No	Yes/No	Yes/No
Bent Little Finger (D): little finger curves in toward other fingers	Yes/No	Yes/No	Yes/No
Attached Earlobes (r): earlobes directly attached to the head	Yes/No	Yes/No	Yes/No
Second Toe Longest (D): second toe is longer than the big toe	Yes/No	Yes/No	Yes/No
Clockwise Whorl (D): hair on the crown of your head turns clockwise	Yes/No	Yes/No	Yes/No
Counterclockwise Whorl (r): hair on the crown of your head turns counterclockwise	Yes/No	Yes/No	Yes/No

Student Instructions: The Developing Baby

Materials Needed

Glue, scissors, colored pencils

How to Create a Right-hand Interactive Notebook Page

Read the Mini-Lesson page. Then cut out the page and attach it to the right-hand page of your interactive notebook. Use what you have learned to create the left-hand page.

How to Create a Left-hand Interactive Notebook Page

Complete the following steps to create the left-hand page of your interactive notebook. Use lots of color.

Step 1: Cut out the title and glue it to the top of the notebook page.

Step 2: Cut out the *Stages of Development* flap book. Apply glue to the back of the gray center and attach the flap book below the title.

Step 3: Cut out the six label pieces. Apply glue to the back of each piece. Attach the correct label to each flap.

Step 4: Under each flap, write a brief summary of the stage of the development.

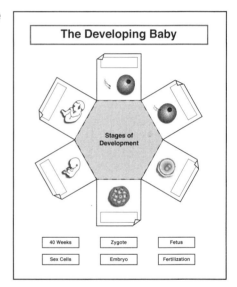

Demonstrate and Reflect on What You Have Learned

Use online or print resources to research fraternal twins. Think about what you learned in the mini-lesson and from your research. In your science notebook, explain the stages of the baby development for fraternal twins.

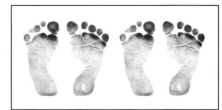

Mini-Lesson

The Developing Baby

In human reproduction, cells from the two parents unite to form a cell that develops into a new human being.

Sex Cells
- Reproductive cells, or **sex cells**, carry the genetic material in the nucleus.
- A sex cell called a **sperm** is produced in the testes of the male.
- A sex cell called an **egg**, or ovum, is produced in the ovaries of a female.

Fertilization
- An egg cell is released from one of the two ovaries.
- The egg travels through the fallopian tube on its way to the uterus.
- A sperm deposited in the vagina travels up the fallopian tube and finds the egg.
- **Fertilization** occurs when the sperm cell unites with the egg by breaking through the membrane of the egg cell.

Zygote
- The new cell formed during fertilization is called a **zygote**. The zygote carries the genetic material from both parents.
- The zygote undergoes cell division, forming two cells. The cells divide over and over again, forming a microscopic ball of cells.

Embryo
- The zygote travels to the uterus where it attaches to the lining of the uterus. The attached zygote is now called an **embryo**.
- The attachment causes the placenta to form. The job of the **placenta** is to exchange nutrients and wastes between the mother and the developing baby.

Pregnancy
- The time a woman carries a developing baby is called **pregnancy**.
- During the first eight weeks, a beating heart develops and the lungs, arms, legs, brain, spinal cord, and nerves begin to form.

Fetus
- After eight weeks, the embryo is called a **fetus**.
- The fetus begins to take on more human features.
- All of the organs begin to form.
- Growth is rapid, and the fetus increases in size.

Baby Is Born
- The baby is fully formed and ready to be born at about 40 weeks.
- During birth, muscle contractions in the uterus force the baby into the birth canal. Contractions continue pushing the baby down the canal and out of the mother through the vagina.

The Developing Baby

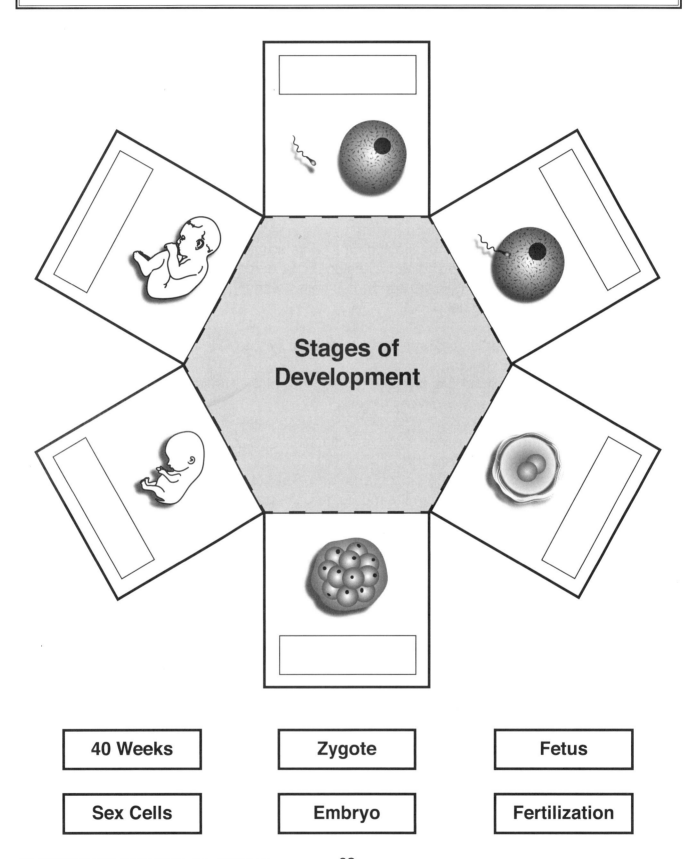

40 Weeks	Zygote	Fetus
Sex Cells	Embryo	Fertilization